~ *Craft Ideas for Your Home* ~

DRAPES AND CURTAINS

~Craft Ideas for Your Home~

DRAPES AND CURTAINS

CANDIE FRANKEL

Little, Brown and Company
Boston   New York   Toronto   London

To Lynne

Acknowledgments

The author gratefully acknowledges the many fine photographers
and designers whose work is featured in these pages.

First edition

ISBN 0-316-28620-6

Library of Congress Catalog Card Number 94-73630

A FRIEDMAN GROUP BOOK

10 9 8 7 6 5 4 3 2 1

Published simultaneously in Canada by Little, Brown & Company (Canada) Limited

CRAFT IDEAS FOR YOUR HOME: DRAPES AND CURTAINS
was prepared and produced by
Michael Friedman Publishing Group
15 West 26th Street
New York, New York 10010

Editor: Elizabeth Viscott Sullivan
Art Director: Jeff Batzli
Designer: Lynne Yeamans
Photography Editor: Colleen Branigan
Production Associate: Camille Lee
Illustrator: Barbara Hennig

Color separations by Fine Arts Repro House Co., Ltd.
Printed in China by Leefung-Asco Printers Ltd.

Contents

~

Introduction

Curtains that billow softly, brilliant stripes that undulate among the drapery folds, voluminous pouf valances that colorfully crown the tops of window frames—these are but a few of the many ways to add drama to home decor. Yet many people are often reluctant to venture beyond traditional curtains and drapes when choosing window treatments, because they fear that creative designs will involve complex measurements, difficult sewing techniques, and added expense. Such misconceptions could not be further from the truth. Some of the most elegant, innovative looks are also the easiest and most affordable to achieve, and are as simple to create as wrapping a length of netting around a curtain pole and letting the ends cascade gracefully to the floor.

Every window in the home can be a showcase for beautiful fabrics and daring design, but successful window treatments must go beyond decoration to enhance a window's function. Windows mediate between the world outdoors and the world within. In warmer climates, uncomplicated drapes and curtains can help streamline the transition between indoor and outdoor living spaces. In colder climates, a lavish layering of shades, drapes, and valances can provide an extra buffer of physical and psychological warmth against chilly nights. A home's architecture and floor plan, its proximity to the street, and how its property is landscaped help define each room's individual needs for privacy, light, and view.

Fortunately, the days are long gone when curtains and drapes were sewn adhering to rigid formulas and had to skirt windowsills and floors at just the right place to be considered correct. Today, designer windows are bursting with spontaneity and delight in taking risks—style trends that are bound to put the novice home sewer at ease. Greater design flexibility also makes it easier to camouflage architectural flaws, such as a ceiling that looms too high or a window that is awkwardly situated. The instructions and illustrations in this section will show you easy ways to sew simple curtains, drapes, and valances as well as how to drape fabric to create no-sew window treatments. By selecting your own fabrics and custom-fitting the styles to the windows in your home, you can readily duplicate professional looks at a fraction of the designer cost.

Tools and Equipment

Making window treatments requires basic sewing equipment and supplies. In addition to fabric, thread, specialty tapes, and hooks, which are discussed in the sections that follow, you will need a sewing machine, pins, scissors, and rulers. A rotary cutter, while not essential, is of great advantage. You will also need a household steam iron and a well-padded ironing board. A brief description of each item follows. If you have never sewn before, or sew only infrequently, the descriptions will help you to assemble the supplies you need and to use them to best advantage.

Sewing Machine All basic curtains, drapes, and shades can be made up neatly and efficiently on a sewing machine. Take time to get acquainted with your machine so that you can thread it, make tension adjustments, and sew forward and backward with ease. Most of your machine stitching will be in straight lines that follow the fabric or tape edge. You can use straight stitching or a blind hem stitch to hem the edges, although sheer panels look neater when sewn with straight stitching. For pucker-free sewing, always use the proper size needle: size 10 (70mm) for lightweight sheers; size 12 (80mm) for medium-weight fabrics such as cotton, linen, and raw silk; and size 14 (90mm) for slightly heavier upholstery and decorator fabrics.

Pins Pins are used to hold pieces of fabric or tape together until they are sewn. A small box of stainless steel pins will see you through many sewing projects. You may prefer to use longer pins, sometimes called quilter's pins, for holding thick or bulky fabrics and tapes. If you draw up your own pleats by hand, pins serve as handy markers. Some pins are manufactured with small, colored plastic or glass heads that make them easier to see and to handle.

Rotary Cutter and Accessories

A rotary cutter consists of a thin, round, razor-sharp blade attached to the end of a plastic handle. To use the cutter, hold it by the handle and roll the wheel-like blade along the fabric surface, cutting through the fabric in one continuous motion. To make straight cuts, roll the blade against the edge of a clear acrylic cutting guide that is imprinted with standard measurements. A self-healing cutting mat should be placed underneath the fabric to protect the tabletop and to provide a firm surface for cutting. Because a rotary cutter can cut through multiple layers of fabric, it can turn out identical panels in a fraction of the time it takes to mark and cut them individually with scissors.

Scissors

Even if you have a rotary cutter, you will still need scissors to cut loose thread ends, trim excess tape, and clip selvages. Scissors should be sharp and should open and close freely. If you plan to do a lot of sewing, you may wish to purchase high-quality sewing shears. Use sewing shears only to cut fabric, never to cut paper or for household chores, in order to avoid dulling the blades.

Rulers

A retractable metal ruler, sold in hardware stores, can be used for all large measurements, from window dimensions to fabric panels. Unlike cloth dressmaker's tapes, the sturdy metal ruler is easier to handle when taking window and wall measurements, and cannot stretch out of shape from use.

A clear plastic ruler will help you fold side and bottom hems evenly. This ruler, printed with an inch or metric grid, can be superimposed on top of the fabric allowance to help you make quick and accurate adjustments.

Sizing Up Your Windows
~

The first step in planning any window treatment is to measure the windows accurately. To begin, draw a rough sketch of each window, including the inside frame, trim, and sill. Even if several windows in a room appear identical or symmetrical, it's important to record separate measurements for each one. Differences may turn up, especially in older homes. If you want to use window treatments for camouflage purposes, precise measurements are critical to achieve the desired effect.

The type of window treatment you are planning will determine which measurements you need to make. Ultimately, you will need only two measurements: the length of the mounted rod or pole and the distance from the rod or pole to the hem of the curtain or drape. If you are uncertain about how you would like to dress the window, record all of the measurements illustrated on this page so that when you do decide, you will have the information at your fingertips. (Sometimes the process of measuring the window frame will inspire ideas for decorating it. Ask a partner to help you, and as you take each measurement, record it on your sketch. Carry your sketch and a pocket calculator with you when you shop for hardware and fabric.)

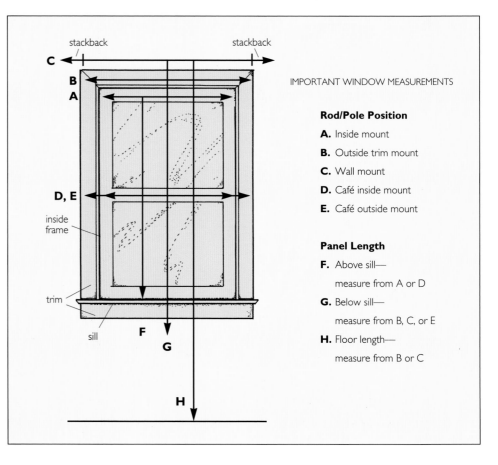

IMPORTANT WINDOW MEASUREMENTS

Rod/Pole Position

A. Inside mount

B. Outside trim mount

C. Wall mount

D. Café inside mount

E. Café outside mount

Panel Length

F. Above sill—
measure from A or D

G. Below sill—
measure from B, C, or E

H. Floor length—
measure from B or C

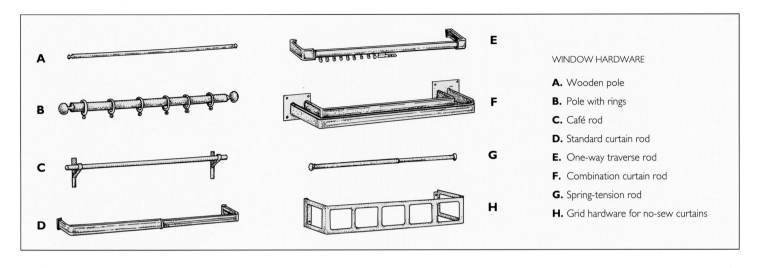

WINDOW HARDWARE

A. Wooden pole

B. Pole with rings

C. Café rod

D. Standard curtain rod

E. One-way traverse rod

F. Combination curtain rod

G. Spring-tension rod

H. Grid hardware for no-sew curtains

Poles, Rods, and Brackets

Curtains and drapes are hung from poles or rods, which are mounted inside, on, or above the window frame with brackets. Collectively, these pieces are called hardware, in contrast to the soft fabric panels that make up the window dressing. There is an enormous variety of window hardware on the market to accommodate many different types of window treatments, and designers frequently improvise their own versions. You can simplify the selection process by deciding first whether your hardware will be decorative or functional.

Decorative hardware is visible, attractive, and integral to the overall look of the window treatment. Examples include brass, wood, and iron poles; poles with rings; sculpted brackets inspired by classical ruins; and found objects, such as tree branches, copper plumbing pipes, and bamboo stems. Designer brackets and finials are generally sold separately, which allows you to assemble your own combinations.

Functional hardware, in contrast, is the backbone of many traditional drapery styles. Designed foremost for utility, not looks, functional rods may or may not be visible in the finished window design. Examples include standard metal or acrylic curtain rods, drapery traverse systems, spring-tension rods that fit inside a window frame, and sash rods that hold panels close to the glass, such as on a French door. Many specialty utility rods have also entered the marketplace: among them are flexible vinyl tubes that curve around Palladian windows; self-bending rods for custom-fitting bay windows; and simple grid systems for draping fabric into swags, rosettes, and poufed tiers without sewing or using drapery hooks.

The hardware you choose depends on the scope of the overall window treatment as well as your personal taste. For drapes that will be open during the day and drawn for privacy in the evening, an easy-gliding traverse rod with pull-cords at one side is the practical choice. If a window looks out on a private patio, stationary drapes entwined around a brass pole can be elegant and adequate. Often, decorative and functional hardware can team up at the same window to provide good looks and convenience. A tab curtain and valance hung from a pretty pole, for example, can readily conceal the work-a-day traverse rod needed for light-filtering privacy sheers.

Choosing Fabric

Many different types of fabric are suitable for window treatments, depending on the style, function, and degree of formality of the room. To choose appropriate fabric for your home, clip photographs of styles and designs that appeal to you from decorating magazines. Study the pictures, looking for similarities between them, and take time to drink in the details. Once you identify a basic look that appeals to you, visit your local fabric store and let your eye wander freely among the displays. You will find that certain colors, textures, and patterns attract your attention more than others.

Beginning sewers usually do best with solid, vertically striped, or small-print fabrics. Unlike large cabbage rose prints, fabrics with solid colors or small design elements can be cut

9

into panels without making extra calculations for pattern matching. Large prints can be difficult in another way, too. They show off to best advantage on smooth, flat expanses, such as on roller shades and walls. Curtains and drapes tend to swallow up large-scale patterns into the folds, for an overall effect that can be both confusing and disappointing. This same "swallowing" works to advantage on striped fabrics by softening the crisp, precise lines.

Once you find several fabrics that you like, unroll each bolt for a yard or so to get a feel for its drape, hang, and tactile qualities. The ideal fabric for most window treatments is firmly woven yet pliable enough to fall into loose folds. Examples include medium-weight cottons, linens, raw silks, rayons, and blends that exhibit both body and drape. Avoid fabrics with a pronounced open weave and soft, fuzzy fibers—they will look limp and droopy when hung. Also avoid heavy-duty upholstery fabrics with a stain-resistant coating, as these may seem rigid and lifeless.

In the sections that follow, you will learn how to use the window measurements you recorded on your sketch (see page 8) to calculate the amount of fabric you will need for specific curtain and drapery styles.

Making Curtains and Drapes

Basic curtains and drapes are very easy to sew, as they are made of straight, rectangular fabric panels that are hemmed or finished at the side and bottom edges. The heading, or top of the panel, can be treated in a variety of ways, depending on how the panel is to be hung. The basics of measuring, cutting, and sewing curtain and drapery panels and their headings also apply to valances and linings.

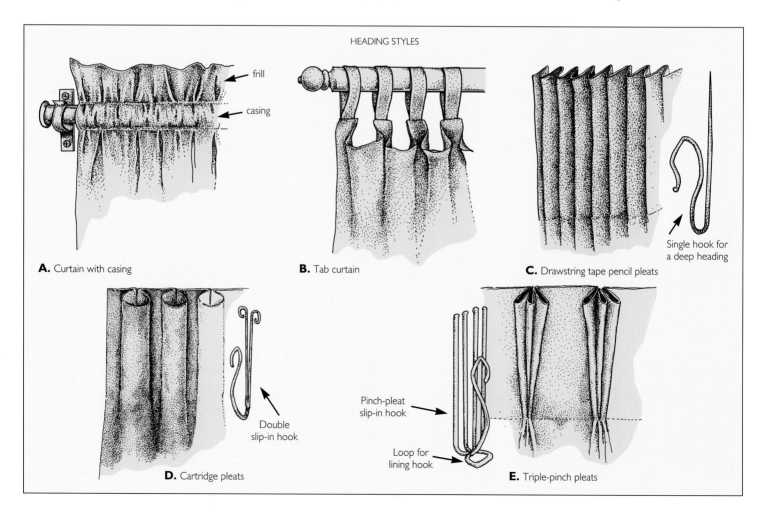

HEADING STYLES

A. Curtain with casing
— frill
— casing

B. Tab curtain

C. Drawstring tape pencil pleats
Single hook for a deep heading

D. Cartridge pleats
Double slip-in hook

E. Triple-pinch pleats
Pinch-pleat slip-in hook
Loop for lining hook

Choosing a Heading Style

The main difference between curtains and drapes is the heading. Curtain headings are sewn with either casings or fabric tabs. A casing is a channel or tunnel through which a rod can be inserted. Tabs are actually loops sewn from the same fabric used for the curtain, although rope, ribbon, and cord make innovative substitutes. Curtain panels hang directly from the rod, and the fabric falls into soft gathers or folds for a relaxed, unstudied look.

Drapes are more formal than curtains. Drapery headings are gathered or pleated using either a special drawstring tape or a pleater tape that is sewn to the wrong side of the fabric. (Pleats also can be folded by hand, although this method is more time-consuming.) Once the drapery heading is made, it is attached to the traverse rod using small hooks, which allow the panels to be opened and closed without disturbing the decorative folds. Each of these four headings—casing, tab, drawstring tape, and pleater tape—has distinctive properties, so be sure to choose a style that will give your curtains or drapes the desired finished look.

Measuring Panels

The first step in making a curtain or drapery panel is to determine its full size, or the finished size before shirring or pleating. Traditional curtains that hang in soft gathers across a window require ample fabric—from two to three times the window width. The full width of the window can be taken up by a single panel, which can be drawn to one side, or by two panels, which can be drawn symmetrically, one to each

---

Calculating Panel Widths

Type of Heading	Full Panel Width*
Casing (sheer fabric)	2½ to 3 x rod length
Casing (medium-weight fabric)	2 to 2½ x rod length
Tab	1½ to 2 x rod length
Drawstring gathers	2 to 2½ x rod length**
Drawstring pencil pleats	3 x rod length**
Cartridge, double, or triple-pinch pleats	2¼ to 2½ x rod length**, or measure from prepleated tape

*Per window; divide by 2 when making two panels per window
**Add 8" to rod length for two-way traverse rods

---

side. The panel length can be short or long. Panels that just graze the windowsill or hang slightly below it create an informal look, while those that touch or pool on the floor set a formal mood.

Panel Width

The full panel width is determined by the rod length and the heading style. Functional curtain rods are generally mounted on the window frame so that the rod length is equal to or slightly larger than the window width. Decorative poles and traverse rods can be mounted directly over the window, or can be extended beyond it on one or both sides to maximize the view when the panels are pulled completely back. The extra rod length required for this fabric "stackback" should be about one-third the window glass width—or enough to accommodate all the tabs or rings when they are pushed together. In some settings, a rod can be mounted along an entire wall to give the illusion of a full-windowed wall, even though the actual window is much smaller. Once you have installed the rod, including any extra for stackback, measure and jot down its full length. You will need to add an extra 8" for two-way traverse rods with master slides that overlap in the center.

Heading style also influences panel width. The chart on this page shows suggested widths based on rod length for different heading styles. As the chart indicates, casing, tab, and drawstring headings allow for some variation, since the gathers can be adjusted looser or tighter to fit the rod.

Pleater tapes are less forgiving, since the hooks are inserted at regular, predetermined intervals and the spaces between the pleats should lie flat when the drape is drawn fully closed. The best way to get an accurate width is to draw up a length of tape into pleats (see page 16) and hang the pleated tape from the rod rings before you sew it to the fabric panel. A single-pronged slip-in hook at each end of the tape will prevent the sides and center overlaps from drooping. Cut off the excess tape 2" beyond each end, mark the pockets that have hooks, then remove the hooks to unpleat the tape. The length of the unpleated tape minus 4" is the full panel width.

Panel Length

Panel length is also affected by variables in the design. The top of the panel can conceal the rod, rise above it in a decorative frill, or hang below it from fabric tabs. (A frill added to a curtain's lower edge means that the basic panels can be cut shorter.) To figure out the appropriate length for your panels, make a sketch of the finished design, including the heading, then work the calculations using the measurements you recorded on your window diagram (page 8). If, for example, length **H** on your window diagram equals 87" and you would like curtains with 3" tabs, the panel length would be 87" minus 3", or 84". A 2" frill would require an extra 2", for 89" total. Adding an extra 8" to 14" at the lower edge will produce curtains that puddle on the floor. Remember, jot in the pertinent measurements on your sketch to keep all the details straight.

Remember, too, that there are no "correct" measurements—the panel size reflects your design decisions, not a rigid formula.

Determining Cut Panel Size

Once you have determined the finished width and length of each panel, you must add heading, side, and hem allowances to obtain the cut panel size. The chart below provides measurement guidelines. Generally, long, formal panels and sheer panels look better with deeper hems, and short, informal panels look better with shorter hems. For a neat, clean appearance—especially desirable on sheers—all hems should be double-folded. The top allowance is determined by the type of heading you choose (see

Allowances for Cut Panel Size

Type of Panel	Heading Allowance	Side Allowance*	Hem Allowance
Sheer curtain with casing	Rod diameter + ¼" to 1¼" ease** + frill depth + ½"	3"	2" to 6" × 2
Opaque curtain with casing	Rod diameter + ¼" to 1¼" ease** + frill depth + ½"	3"	2" to 4" × 2
Tab curtain	½" + 2" to 4" + 1"	3"	2" to 4" × 2
Drawstring gathers	Frill depth + ¼"	3"	2" to 4" × 2; additional length for sheers
Drawstring pencil pleats	½"	3"	2" to 4" × 2; additional length for sheers
Pleater-tape heading	½"	3"	2" to 4" × 2; not recommended for sheers
With sewn-in lining	Depends on heading	2"	2" to 4" × 2

*Per side; multiply by 2 for total allowance per panel   **Minimum allowance; larger rods require more ease

pages 14–17). Casing widths will vary, depending on rod diameter and frill depth. Extra-wide panels and heavier fabrics need wider casings to shirr evenly without bunching.

After you decide on appropriate allowances, jot down the figures on your sketch and tally up the overall width and length to obtain the cut panel size. You can always allow more fabric than necessary when cutting the panels to give yourself room to experiment with a deeper frill or casing. Any excess can be trimmed off later or taken up in a deeper hem.

Buying and Cutting Fabric

Once you have determined the cut panel size, you can calculate how much fabric to buy. Curtain and drapery panels are typically cut so that their vertical drop corresponds to the length of the goods. Often, you will be able to fit one panel width between the two selvages. Suppose, for example, that you need to cut two panels 38" wide by 48" long and the fabric you have chosen is 45" wide. You will be able to fit one panel across the width of the fabric with 7" to spare, and you will need a fabric length of two times 48", or 96". Keeping in mind that the suggested width for curtains and drawstring-tape drapes is a range rather than a precise figure, you may want to simply incorporate the extra 7" into the panel for fuller gathers. Or, you could use the leftover fabric to make tabs or tiebacks.

When windows are large and the panel width exceeds the fabric width, you will need to cut several separate sections and sew them together. The sections can be the same size or different sizes. Work out a plan for piecing

Making Drapes and Curtains

A STEP-BY-STEP CHECKLIST

~

1. Measure the window and determine the finished panel size.

2. Add side, hem, and heading allowances to determine the cut panel size.

3. Use the cut panel size to determine the amount of fabric needed.

4. Cut out the panels from the fabric.

5. Sew the side allowances, headings, and hems.

your panels, so that the wider sections will fall near the center of the window wall and any narrower sections will be at the sides. To make a 138"-wide panel, for example, you can join two 56"-wide sections and one 26"-wide section. Add 3" side allowances to the two outer edges and ¾" to all the inner edges to obtain the cut width of each section, keeping in mind that the cut width cannot exceed the fabric width. In our example, shown below, the three 80"-long sections (the widest one is 59¾") can each be cut from 60"-wide fabric, and the total fabric length required is 3 times 80", or 240".

After you calculate the length of fabric you need, always add 10 percent to allow for shrinkage. An extra half yard (or half meter) should be enough to make matching tab headings or tiebacks. Washable fabrics should be preshrunk by washing, drying, and pressing them just as you would the finished curtains. If the fabric has been treated to resist soiling or wrinkling, however, be aware that washing may remove

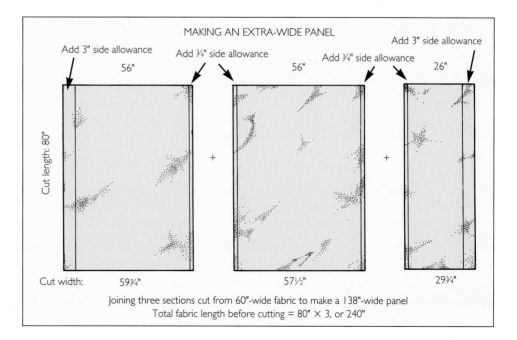

MAKING AN EXTRA-WIDE PANEL

Add 3" side allowance   Add ¾" side allowance   Add ¾" side allowance   Add 3" side allowance

56"   56"   26"

Cut length: 80"

+   +

Cut width: 59¾"   57½"   29¾"

Joining three sections cut from 60"-wide fabric to make a 138"-wide panel
Total fabric length before cutting = 80" × 3, or 240"

Sewing French Seams
~

To give extra-wide panels a neat finish on both the right and wrong sides, join the sections using French seams. Although the French seam is particularly suited to sheers, it works well with other fabrics, too.

To sew the seam, place the fabric pieces together, wrong sides facing and edges matching. Stitch the seam ½" from the edge, then trim the allowance ⅛" from the stitching. Fold the fabric along the seam line, right sides facing. Stitch again through both layers, ¼" from the folded edge. On the wrong side, press the seam first to one side and then to the other. The finished seam will look like a traditional seam from the right side.

protective finishes and sizings. It is important to buy all the fabric from one bolt to avoid mixing dye lots.

To cut the panels accurately, smooth out the fabric on a large work surface. Clip the selvages every 3" so that the fabric lies flat without puckering. Draw out a crosswise thread at one end from selvage to selvage, then cut straight across on this line to mark the edge of the first panel. Don't neglect this step, for if the panels are cut off-grain, they will never hang straight, no matter how much you press them or try to

coax them into position. Using a clear plastic ruler or triangle to square up the corners, cut all the panels to the proper size. If you wish, you can fold the fabric and cut several panels at a time with a rotary cutter.

Sewing Fabric

Curtain and drapery panels that are cut true to the fabric grain are a pleasure to sew. Use a compatible sewing thread—cotton thread for cottons, linens, and natural fibers; silk thread for silks; and polyester thread for synthetic blends—in a color that matches the background color of the panel fabric. Thread the sewing machine and set the stitch length for 6 to 8 stitches per inch (2 to 3 stitches per cm) for sheers, to 10 stitches per inch (3 to 4 stitches per cm) for opaque fabrics. Test the stitching on a scrap of the panel fabric; adjust the machine tension if the stitching pulls or puckers.

When making casing and tape headings, sew the side allowances first, then the heading, then the lower hem. For tab headings, sew the tabs and headings first, then the sides and the hem. If a precise hem length is not important to the design, you may want to follow the lead of mass-market drapery manufacturers and sew the hem first, then the sides and heading. Whichever order you choose, proceed assembly-line style, completing like steps for each panel before moving to the next step.

Sewing Side Hems
Fold each side edge of the panel 1½" to the wrong side, then 1½" to the wrong side again. For professional results, use a clear plastic ruler to measure the allowances, then pin or baste the folds in place. You can press the folded edges, but be

careful not to move the iron back and forth, as this may stretch the fabric. Straight-stitch or blind-hem-stitch close to the inner folded edge on the wrong side to secure the hem. The 1½" finished width is a standard width suitable for most fabrics, but you can allow for wider or narrower hems when planning the cut size.

Sewing Headings
Before you sew headings, make sure all the panels in the set are facing the same direction. You don't want a printed design or a brushed velvet surface to appear upside down on one of the panels!

Casing Heading

A casing is made by folding a deep hem along the top edge of the curtain panel and making two rows of stitching, one along the inner fold and one a short distance above it. (The bit of excess fabric above the top row of stitching will gather up on the rod, forming an attractive frill. If you wish, you can use just one row of stitching and omit the frill.)

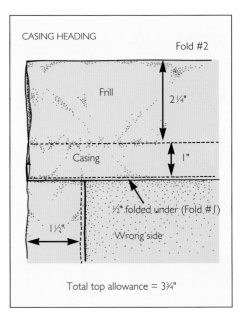

CASING HEADING

Fold #2

Frill

2¼"

Casing

1"

½" folded under (Fold #1)

1½"

Wrong side

Total top allowance = 3¾"

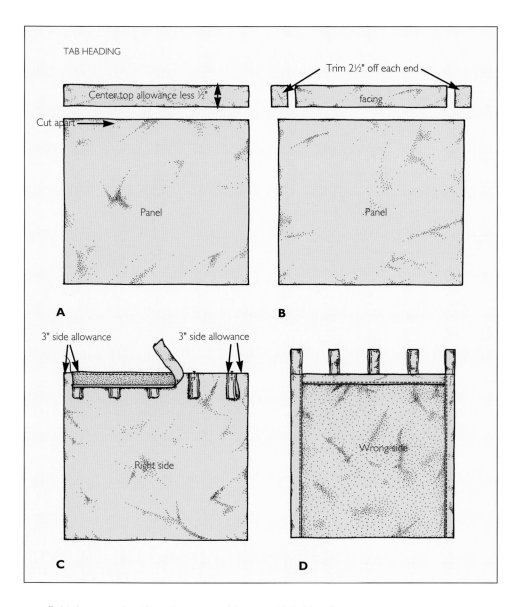

TAB HEADING

Center top allowance less ½"

Cut apart →

Panel

A

Trim 2½" off each end

facing

Panel

B

3" side allowance   3" side allowance

Right side

C

Wrong side

D

Fold the raw edge ½" to the wrong side, then bring the folded edge down for the predetermined allowance recorded on your diagram to make Fold #2. Straight-stitch along the first fold through all the layers to form the bottom of the casing, then stitch a second parallel row above it to make the proper width casing. Backtack the beginning and end of each row to secure the stitches. Slide the curtain rod into the casing and shirr the panel on the rod.

Tab Heading

To sew a tab heading, you must decide on the finished tab width, height, and spacing. Most tabs are ½" to 2" wide and extend 2" to 6" above the top of the panel, depending on the diameter of the pole and the length of the panel. Tabs are spaced 4" to 8" apart; generally, the larger the tab, the greater the spacing. If you have trouble visualizing an appropriate size, cut a sample panel and tabs from plain paper or scrap material, and pin them together over the rod you will be using; adjust the size until you achieve the desired effect. To calculate the number of tabs per panel, divide the finished panel width by the tab spacing and round that figure to the nearest whole number. A 38" panel with tabs about 5" apart, for example, would require eight tabs.

To make the tabs, cut two strips of fabric, one ¼" wider and the other ¾" wider than the finished tab. For 1½" tabs, for example, you would cut one 1¾"-wide strip and one 2¼"-wide strip. If the curtain fabric is thick or bulky, cut the narrower strip from a coordinating lightweight fabric. Sew the strips together, right sides facing, along the long edges, so that the wider strip buckles. Turn the resulting tube right side out and press it flat so that both seams fall on the same side. Cut the tube into individual lengths that are equal to two times the finished tab height plus 1". The strip for a 3" tab height, for example, would be 7" long. Continue making tabs until you have the amount you need.

To reduce bulk, tabs are attached before side allowances are sewn. Place the curtain panel right side up on a flat surface. Using a rotary cutter and a clear ruler, trim off the top allowance minus ½" (A). Trim 2½" off each end of this piece (B), then press one long edge ½" to the wrong side to make a facing. Fold each tab in half crosswise, seams inside, and pin the ends together. Next, pin the tabs evenly across the top of the panel, edges matching and with the 3" allowances extending at each side. Center the facing on top, right side down and long edges matching; the side edges of the facing will not reach the edges of the panel. Stitch ½" from the long edge through all layers (C). Turn and press the facing to the wrong side so

15

the tabs pop up. Straight-stitch or blind-hem-stitch the lower facing edge in place. Finish the side allowances as above (D).

Drawstring-Tape Heading

A drawstring tape is a fabric tape with two or more cords threaded through evenly spaced eyelets. Tapes range from 1" wide, for soft gathers, to 3" or deeper, for slender, elegant pencil pleats across the header.

To attach a drawstring tape, lay the panel on a flat surface, wrong side up. Fold down the top edge the depth of the frill plus ¼" and pin. Cut a length of tape 4" longer than the panel width. Carefully pull out the drawstrings by 1" to 2" at one end and tie them together in a secure knot on the wrong side. Trim off the cord ends,

trim the tape ⅝" from the knot, and press the tape end to the wrong side (A). Lay the tape, knot side down, along the heading so that the top edge overlaps the raw edge by ¼" and the folded end butts the side hem. Baste the top and bottom edges of the tape to the panel, trimming and folding the free end neatly to the inside. Allow the excess drawstring to extend freely. Machine-stitch along the top and bottom edges of the tape through all the layers (B).

When you finish sewing, pull the free drawstrings, drawing up the heading tightly, then release the gathers until the heading width matches the traverse rod length. Tie the loose cord ends in a secure knot. You can cut off the excess cord, or you can leave the cord ends long in order to release the gathers when the panels need cleaning and pressing. Count the number of rings in the traverse rod, then insert a corresponding number of double-ended drapery hooks along the exposed cord at even intervals to hang the drapery. Drapes that have two panels should be hung with the concealed knots in the center.

Pleater-Tape Heading

Pleater tape is a stiff buckram tape, about 3" wide, that has slender vertical pockets woven at evenly spaced intervals. The pleats are formed by inserting slip-in hooks into the pockets at evenly spaced intervals. The number of prongs determines the pleat style.

To attach pleater tape, lay the panel on a flat surface, right side up. Cut a length of pleater tape 4" longer than the panel width. Place the tape across the heading, pocket side down and top edges matching, so that the tape ends extend 2" on each side. Stitch ¼" from the top edge through both layers (many tapes feature a

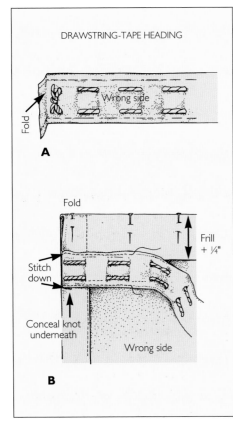

DRAWSTRING-TAPE HEADING

A — Fold, Wrong side

B — Fold, Frill + ¼", Stitch down, Conceal knot underneath, Wrong side

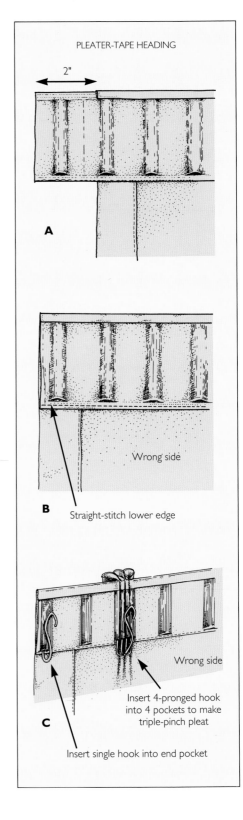

PLEATER-TAPE HEADING

2"

A

B — Wrong side, Straight-stitch lower edge

C — Wrong side, Insert 4-pronged hook into 4 pockets to make triple-pinch pleat, Insert single hook into end pocket

contrasting thread guideline for stitching). Turn the tape to the wrong side, forming a stiff upper edge and concealing the seam (A). Fold the excess tape to the inside, then straight-stitch the tape to the panel along the lower edge through both layers (B). To make the pleats, insert the hook ends into the pockets (C).

Sewing Hems

When the heading is complete and the panels are hung, measure and pin up double hems at the lower edges. Let the curtains hang for a few days, then check the hem length to make sure the panels haven't stretched; if they have, you'll need to readjust the length. Take down the panels to sew the hems. To help drapes hang evenly, small flat weights resembling washers can be sewn into the lower corners inside the hem on the wrong side of the panel.

Adding a Lining

Draperies that are lined have an air of luxury. Linings add body and insulation, help ensure privacy, and screen harsh sunlight that can cause delicate fabrics to fade. Linings are traditionally sewn of natural-colored muslin or cotton, but decorative fabrics can be used as well. Generally, the lining should be made of a lighter-weight fabric than the drapery. There are two basic types of linings: detachable and sewn-in.

Detachable Linings

Detachable linings are suitable when the drapery and lining fabrics have different cleaning requirements. The lining panel is gathered using lining tape. The length and width of a lining panel depends on the type of lining tape you choose and the fullness of the gathers, but the dimensions are

calculated using the same principles as for drapes. The finished lining is joined to the drapery with special hooks: one end of the hook grabs onto the lining heading, while the other end slips onto a lower loop in the drapery heading hook. This allows the lining heading to hang below the drapery heading, reducing excess bulk. Some traverse rods have a second set of rings built in to hold the lining hooks.

Sewn-In Linings

Sewn-in linings give drapery panels a neat, clean finish along the side edges. For a traditional sewn-in lining that shows 1½" of drapery fabric on the wrong side before the lining begins, cut the drapery panel with a 2" allowance instead of the usual 3" on each side. Cut the lining panel to measure 6" less than the drapery panel's cut width. Sew the two panels together, wrong sides out, down the sides, then turn them right side out on a flat surface and baste the top edges together so that both seams fall 1½" from each side edge. You can also cut the panels the same size so that the seams fall at the edges for a completely reversible look.

To finish lined panels, sew the heading as usual, then hang the panels for several days before hemming. If you prefer, the lining can be cut without the topmost allowance to prevent the frill from becoming too bulky. To ensure even hanging, hem the lining and main panel separately.

Valances

A valance, an accent curtain that runs across the top of a window, can be used to conceal the workings of a traverse rod or can stand on its own above a café curtain or roller shade.

Classically styled val[...] exactly the same way as [...] they accent. The heading [...] rod, sewn with tabs, o[...] using tapes. The finishe[...] be about one-eighth the [...] length. To calculate the cut valance size, add side, heading, and hem allowances just as you would for larger panels.

The pouf valance is an easy-to-make style that requires just three rows of straight stitching. Cut a piece of fabric 2½ times the desired finished depth, including the frill, by 2½ times the window width. Sew the long edges together to make a tube, turn right side out, and press the raw edges at each end 1" to the inside. Lay the tube flat, with the seam at the back. Sew two rows of stitching through both layers to make a casing and a frill (see the chart on page 11 to calculate the casing width). Shirr the valance on the rod, then stuff crumpled newsprint or bubble wrap through the side openings until the valance is full and puffy. After you set the rod on the brackets, adjust the fabric at the sides to conceal the openings.

No-Sew Draping and Shaping

One of the easiest ways to dress a window is by draping a length of fabric around a pole or arranging it around special gridded hardware. The results mimic the detail-rich swags, rosettes, and double-lined styles of the late nineteenth century, without tedious measuring or tailoring. No-sew styles are easy and quick to arrange and are readily removed for cleaning or to change colors. The drawback is that they are stationary—that is, you cannot move them back and forth along a track to control the light or view. To make a no-sew swag more practical, you can always back it with privacy drapes attached to a traverse rod.

Pole and Bracket Draping

There are many innovative ways to drape or wrap a long length of fabric around a pole. For the best results, choose a soft, pliable fabric that falls easily into loose folds. Sheers, laces, and thin, crunchy fabrics, such as taffeta, also work well. You do not need to finish the selvage edges, as these will be coaxed under by hand as you arrange the drape. Short drapes should be hemmed, but the raw edges of long drapes that puddle on the floor can simply be tucked under to hide them from view. For a two-tone effect, sew two different fabrics of equal lengths together along the selvages to make a tube. As the tube is twisted and wrapped around the pole, each color will show in turn.

The illustrations shown on this page demonstrate some of the ways to drape and wrap fabric around poles and brackets. To determine how much fabric you will need, work out your basic design using a length of stout cord. Measure the cord, then factor in a hem allowance and a 10 percent shrinkage allowance to obtain the total length to purchase. If you plan to dress a number of windows, a long length of fabric will let you try out different styles inexpensively. Once you arrange a style, pushpins, staples, or Velcro fasteners can help slippery fabrics stay in place.

18

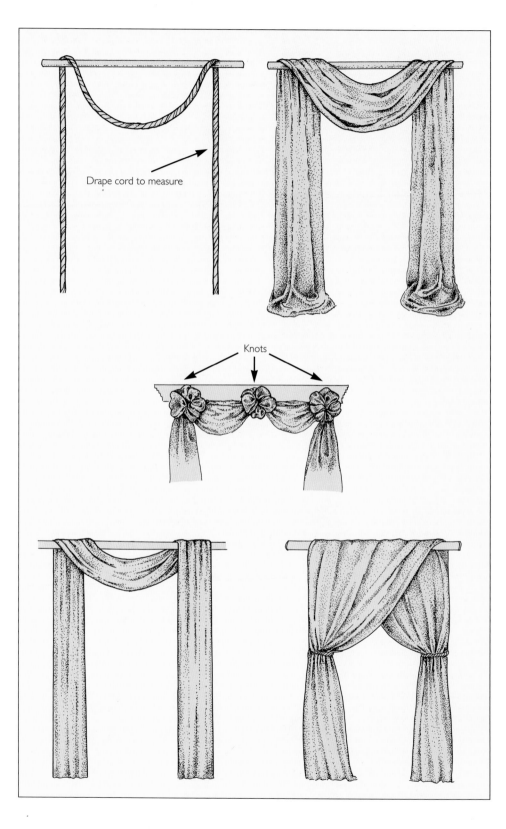

Drape cord to measure

Knots

Using Grid Hardware

Grid-based hardware systems are available in a variety of sizes at home decorating centers, at department stores, and through mail-order catalogs. Every manufacturer's product is a little bit different, so follow the package instructions for purchasing the proper amount of fabric and for mounting and using the grid. Once the fabric has been inserted, the grid holds it securely in place—without sewing, hooks, or tapes. Thus grid hardware enables you to remove the fabric just as easily for a change of color or style.

~

The photographs in the chapters that follow illustrate the many ways curtains, drapes, and shades can team together to create eye-catching windows for every room in your home. You will see traditional designs that bathe a room with sumptuous elegance, dramatic swags and poufs that take little or no sewing, and unusual yet practical solutions for problem windows. Regardless of your decor and the size of your budget, you will find inspiration for window treatments that can make your home more livable, inviting, and uniquely yours.

~

PART ONE

Visions of Grandeur

THE WELL-DRESSED WINDOW

though, state-of-the-art hardware ensures that even the most romantic styles function with modern efficiency.

Traditional curtains, drapes, and shades are perennial favorites in home decor. They bestow a sense of order, balance, and symmetry upon a room, even when the furnishings are eclectic or offbeat. As if by magic, drapes and curtains can transform a boxy, nondescript room into a cozy study or a sumptuous bedroom retreat—testimony to the suggestive power of decorative art.

The photographs in this section showcase classic drapes and curtains in a variety of settings.

*J*ust a few centuries ago, beautiful fabric that draped around windows was a luxury only the well-to-do could afford, but today those styles are the mainstays of decorating in ordinary homes. Long, flowing drapes, generous valances, and perky swags and tails are easy to create, yet exude the gracious warmth and civility of a grander, more formal age. Behind the scenes, Included are period rooms, contemporary city apartments, and country houses. Some of the styles are direct copies of historical designs, while others are creative adaptations using today's newest fabrics and decorator trims. All show the strong lines, satisfying proportions, and love of color and texture that make a room well dressed, even for every day.

~

Left: *Spilling in through a tall, gracefully arched window, natural daylight is an unexpected bonus in the modest vestibule of this older home. Instead of a dark, serious curtain, which would compromise the light, a golden yellow fabric gently filters it, imbuing the small space with a warm, amber glow. The puddled fabric lends an element of surprise and sophistication as well.*

21

~

~

Opposite: *Like nineteenth-century ladies' gowns, classical window dressings revel in yards of fabric and trims that are arranged into voluptuous folds, gathers, and shapely curves. At this living room window, a dramatic interplay of three different fabrics suggests the proscenium curtain of an old theater or opera house and is in keeping with the formality of the room without being overwhelming.*

Right: Despite this room's formal underpinnings, the presence of a plantation chair, music corner, and marble statue of a woman in repose inspires a relaxed mood. In keeping with the spare yet elegant look, a bright red formal valance, its graceful swags caught up in tricorn pleats, is the sole adornment on a full-length window. The lack of additional drapery, which would detract from the room's uncluttered ambience, enables light to spill into the room, thus inspiring a feeling of warmth.

22

Left: Asymmetrical draperies in mirror image visually transform these two side-by-side windows, making them appear as a single architectural feature and adding a contemporary element to this gracious parlor. The windows originally had separate sets of draperies that together made a heavy backdrop for the empire sofa, dwarfing its dainty lines before dropping out of sight behind the curved backrest. The two new window dressings elegantly resolve the disharmonious proportions, cascading around the sofa on each side and placing it center stage.

Left: Coordinating a room's color scheme around its upholstered furniture is a traditional and practically foolproof decorating approach. Here, the red and creamy white striped fabric covering a curvaceous settee is matched by a stunning window treatment secured with a gold cord on one side and an ornamental brass tieback on the other. The asymmetry of both the window treatment and the settee play beautifully against each other, while a red and gold medallion border runs a predictable course around the room just under the cornice. To provide privacy, an unadorned white shade pulls down behind the window treatment without intruding upon the decor.

Right: Drapery ensembles that combine light- and dark-colored fabrics perform the twofold task of admitting light and securing privacy. Forming a backdrop for a collection of photographs, the sheer white drapery installed in the living room of this home can be drawn open during the day for a view of the garden or closed for light-filtering privacy. At night, additional privacy can be gained by releasing the tiebacks and letting the navy blue drapes fall closed over the sheer panel.

Below: Often used to add graphic interest to interior decor, striped fabrics take on a soft, flexible appearance when caught up in curtain or drapery folds. In a room used as a nursery, the same striped fabric selected for the long curtain panels also appears on a round tablecloth, which brings the crisp stripes back into focus. The blue and white palette makes a ready backdrop for perky red accents, such as a red gingham lamp shade, crib linens with red and blue appliqués, and a vase of fresh tulips.

Above: When architectural details appear too rigid or geometric, a curtain can quickly and inexpensively soften their overall impact. This front entryway enjoys a dramatic view through a gridwork of small windows encased in massive redwood doors. Left unadorned, the doors are imposing and the view appears aloof and unrelated to the interior. The solution: adding curtains on each side to help frame the vista while giving the interior a cozier, more sheltered ambience. To visitors approaching the home, the curtains extend a note of welcome.

~

Above: Architecture doesn't always have to inspire decor. In the living room of this city apartment, one might expect to find minimalist decor and vertical blinds covering the sleek, contemporary windows. Instead, balloon shades billow across the two windows, their poufed volume and signature scallops softening the look of this traditional room. Each window's shade can be raised and lowered independently, but the close side-by-side placement creates the illusion of a single tier.

~

Left: With ingenious artifice, the draperies flanking a real window were duplicated and hung in various locations throughout this dining room to give the illusion of more windows than are actually present. Adorned with the same persimmon-colored draperies as the window at the left, the area behind the ornamental statue is actually a mirror. Additional panels were hung on the wall behind the buffet as well. The effect is rich and opulent.

~

Right: The living room in this home reverses the usual roles of light walls and darker drapery by placing light buttery yellow fabric against a dark forest green wall. The use of yellow—suggested by three prints atop a faux bow, all applied by decoupage directly onto the wall—extends its influence to a pleated shade and window muntins in this carefully coordinated scheme. The drapery fabric has a slight sheen but is otherwise plain, a dramatic contrast to the subtler, two-tone floral green wallpaper that resembles brocade.

28

~

Right: When a soaring ceiling is a room's crowning glory, valances that draw the eye upward are a must. In this tastefully furnished living room, the tails of each double-swag valance achieve this effect by their sheer ornateness, as they are gathered up into generous poufs. A painting of a sailing vessel nestled in between the swags balances their frilliness by conjuring up thoughts of adventure.

Left: Even if screening an unwanted view is the primary job of a curtain, its decorative potential should not be ignored. In this wood-paneled sitting room, floral prints were already well represented, so a large gingham check was used for the stationary sash curtains. Mounted on the lower half of each window, the sash curtains impart a publike atmosphere that is cozy and secure. A floral-print balloon shade covers the top half of one window, but the other is left unadorned to show off its thick-textured leaded glass.

Below: Traditionally sheer and white, Austrian shades take on a new personality when sewn from a lively striped fabric. Their sunny orange and olive hues suggest an awning at a beach or poolside cabana, lending a decidedly informal air to a living room furnished in an oriental mode. The shade construction softens the stripes naturally so that they don't appear angular or geometric.

Above: Sheer curtains add a lovely, delicate quality to a room, but they also run the risk of appearing too ethereal, without clear definition. In this dark, masculine bedroom furnished with antiques, a compromise is deftly arranged by edging each sheer curtain panel with a delicate yet slightly weighty contrasting trim. The trim makes the gentle crisscross of the curtain panels visible and helps the sheer white fabric relate more closely to the floral-print cornices above.

~

Above: Washed in fiery red and terra-cotta hues, an Arts and Crafts living room called out for some cool

color relief. The solution was a compatible olive green, introduced in the floral-print sofa and given

fuller exposure in floor-skimming curtains. Shimmering and slightly crunchy in texture, the curtain fabric adds

a touch of elegance to the no-nonsense, utilitarian furnishings and custom-crafted fireplace surround.

~

Right: When the same fabric is used for both drapery and upholstery, a room's decor runs the risk of appearing stilted and uninspired. Forestalling any predictability here, a pretty pink and red floral print on a powder blue background always looks cheerful and inviting. Generously shirred for the drapery panels and valance, the fabric shows a smooth, taut face on the upholstered armchair. A companion oval-backed chair, upholstered in a compatible but not identical shade of blue, studiously avoids the matched-set syndrome.

32
~

Right: Adding a valance is the easiest way to make a window appear taller than it actually is. This amply gathered valance, sewn from an attractive green and off-white miniature upholstery print, hides the bare wall above the window frame as well as the drapery hardware. Hung lower, the valance would make the window appear less lofty and allow less light to enter the room.

Left: Used generously, a pretty fabric can make an entire room, not just the windows, look special. This charming bedroom was created around a pink and pale aqua floral print, which appears in the draperies, the bed's half-tester canopy, and the wall covering. Rather than overwhelm the room, the fabric's soothing pastel colors and gentle pattern seem to envelop and protect it, creating an illusory but pampering indoor flower garden.

~

Below: *Light, airy, and gossamer-thin, sheer curtains rely on subtle rather than demonstrative touches to enhance a decor. Here, a sheer panel that is machine-loomed with delicate floral patterns forms a lovely backdrop for a feminine dressing table. Plain sheers would have been just as serviceable but far less enticing when viewed against the vanity skirt's lacy inset and the mirror's filigree frame.*

~

Above: *Finding a window treatment that would accentuate rather than truncate this Palladian arch posed a difficult decorating challenge. The solution was a flexible vinyl curtain rod that rises above the window in a gentle semicircle. The floral-print panels attached to it were pulled to each side, just brushing but not obscuring the window's crowning arch. Elegant yet simply conceived, the new curtain shows off the window's classical architectural lines yet does not block the light from entering the stairwell and landing.*

~

$\mathscr{L}eft$: Overly fussy or colorful window dressings generally look out of place in rooms with clean architectural lines and minimal furniture. Here, simple pinch-pleated curtains hang alongside a casement window, calling attention to the lush garden view beyond. Monotone but not austere, the creamy hues of the curtain and wall echo the bleached wood of the dining table and chairs. Designed to showcase the garden foliage, the room's decor uses green, gray, and black as its sole accent colors.

35

~

~

Simply Special

EASY TO MAKE, EASY TO LIVE WITH

For people who lead busy lives or who relocate every few years, simplicity is the key to successful nesting. For those who are not confident sewers or who wish to make a temporary home more inviting, or who want quick and easy solutions, no-sew window treatments—created in a short time by arranging lengths of unhemmed, unfinished fabric around drapery poles or brackets—are the answer. Far from being makeshift, such styles offer a way to redis-

cover the fluid lines and graceful folds that are characteristic of all beautiful drapery design. The results are fresh, spontaneous, unassuming, and undeniably appealing to the modern sensibility.

No-sew styles have another advantage: they are easy to create. Their accessibility has made them popular, even for permanent residences. There are no right or wrong methods, only free experimentation with the bonus of instant gratification. Adjustments take just a few moments, and you can always start from scratch to work out a new arrangement. The photographs in this section present no-sew or easy-sew styles that can be readily adapted for various fabrics. The relaxed attitude of the window treatments shown here suits today's informal lifestyle, yet still manages to carry all the glamour and good lines of the traditional window dressings that inspired these looks.

~

Left: *These leaded-glass diamond-shaped panes are a detail to show off, not conceal behind a window treatment. One option is to tack a stationary swag into a position that does not obscure the panes. Confidently pleated, the swags shown here are worthy accents for the understated beige and green decor.*

37

~

Opposite: *Situated at right angles to one another in a corner of a room, a tall arched window and a built-in Romanesque niche each clamored to be the center of attention. To resolve the tension, a spotlight was installed inside the niche to highlight its faux marbling, while the window's symmetry was played down by draping a length of dull green sheer fabric casually across the window frame. One side of the fabric was gathered up with a gold cord in an impromptu arrangement, a further effort to distinguish the two arches from one another.*

Below: In a weekend house, decorating results should come quickly and easily, without hours of labor spent at the sewing machine or fussing over details. Here, a semicircular enclosed porch cried out for a window treatment that was dressier than roller shades but just as simple to install. A bit of playful experimentation with many yards of sheer white fabric resulted in a romantic knotted valance design that can be thumbtacked or stapled to the window frame. Above each window, a small stenciled angel guards the serene scene with watchful eyes.

Above: Draped across ornamental tiebacks that are mounted at the top corners of each window frame, turquoise swags flirtatiously reveal a hint of golden lining behind their generous folds. Similar turquoise and gold hues dominate the room, appearing in the carpet, walls, upholstered chairs, and a bed tester, which is visible in the cheval glass. Crisscross sheers take their color cue from the white dado, which provides a refreshing interlude from the turquoise and gold intensity yet does not diminish the dramatic color scheme.

$\mathcal{L}eft:$ *Susceptible to sudden gusts of wind, a light curtain in an open porch doorway can billow about and make egress difficult. A single overhand knot, tied at door-lever height, is a quick and stylish remedy. Easy to grab, the knot can be held aside for graceful entrances and exits. Knotting a panel creates a slender silhouette that grants more of an outside view as well.*

39

Right: In cities where the streets run like caverns between tall buildings, natural daylight in an apartment is a precious commodity. To preserve every particle of light entering this penthouse salon, a sheer panel was draped over a long rod and hung to cover as little of the window wall as possible. Requiring no sewing, the soft curves of the panel lend warmth to the room and can be rearranged into a new configuration—either symmetrical or irregular—at any time.

40

~

Below: *Drape a square of fabric over a pole and voilà—instant valance. This eclectically appointed bathroom has a window instead of the customary mirror directly above the basin, and the deep sill is filled with assorted oddments, including marble busts, notes and papers, perfume bottles, hairbrushes, and a few stems of a pink flowering plant. The impromptu valance serves to frame the assemblage and provides a bit of bohemian-style privacy as well.*

41

~

Above: *Filling in for a nonexistent wall, a curtain installed for privacy glides open and closed on small metal rings at a moment's notice. Not intended to provide total seclusion, a curtain like this can be used to screen off a dressing, sleeping, or storage area, to hide clutter, or to partition a loft into living and work areas. Long tabs and a generous panel width resulted in the reverse scalloping at the heading.*

Below: When a room is ripe for renovation, sample curtain or drapery panels hung at the windows can make it easier to assess how daylight enters the area throughout the day and inspire ideas for the future decor. In this old house, the afternoon light filters through gossamer-thin curtains, the strongest beams spotlighting an old wrought iron tête-à-tête garden chair that awaits a new home. Easy to hang, the curtain helps cheer up the room until the remodeling can begin.

Above: The old-fashioned utility sink at this country home was so quirky and fun to use that it called for a window treatment in the same spirit. Lengths of gauzy fabric were hung in free-form swags, then crowned with an arrangement of dried twigs, flowers, and grasses. Unlike a café curtain, which covers the lower half of a window, this artistic creation gives those who use the sink a clear view of the unspoiled landscape.

~

Left: Steps off a dining room, this stone balcony extends a home's living space to the outdoors. The sliding glass doors of the dining room are flanked by long curtains, which create a tantalizing juxtaposition between the indoor and outdoor areas as they camouflage the doors' metal framework. The curtains' neutral beige fabric was a good choice, as it introduces the outdoor garden view, then quietly recedes from the limelight.

43

~

~

Right: Contemporary
dwellings often feature
dramatic expanses of glass
that make ready canvases
for draping fabric creatively. In
this dining room, large black
poles mounted just below the
ceiling accept yards of sheer
chiffon, which falls gently and
casually across the window.
Passersby see a similar view,
although a garden wall
prevents them from gazing in
through the lower half of
the window.

44

~

~

Below: Sometimes found objects can support a swag just as readily as purchased hardware. In a dining room filled with country furniture, paintings, and crockery, small grapevine wreaths perform a useful service as rings to hold blue-gray swags. Originally purchased as decorations for cupboard doors, the wreaths are an asset to the look of the room, and their rough texture helps prevent the slippery swag fabric from sliding about as well.

~

Above: When windows are not the main point of interest, they should be dressed simply and unobtrusively to avoid competing with a room's more decorative assets. In this charming colonial dining room, a hand-painted mural offers a sweeping panorama of life along a riverbank, while an oriental carpet puts intricate patterns and vivid colors underfoot. Gracefully taking a backseat, the window swags are adequate but not voluminous, and their quiet green and white print blends amicably with the landscape view.

45

~

Below: A deep green dado and a creamy white wall created a strong dark-light demarcation in the living room of this Tudor-style home. To help the two "halves" of the room relate better to one another, printed cotton draperies run down the wall, puddling on the carpet-covered wood floor. The drapery folds, gentle swags, and soft print impart a romantic aura and help tone down the room's masculine feeling.

Above: Curtains do not always need a window to work their magic. Here, a daybed alcove is made cozier by two stationary curtains that are tacked to the crossboard above it. The curtain fabric is also used for the bed linens and shirred panel, coordinating with the striped sofa upholstery and the grape-leaf wallpaper. Against this mélange of patterns, the windows in this comfortable bed-sitting room are minimally dressed with a few white table linens. Filling in for valances, the linens are starched, pressed, and tacked to the upper window frames, affording an unobstructed view of the backyard garden.

~

Above: A room that faces onto a busy street presents special needs for privacy. In this
country-style living room, decorated with black, gold, and white checks and a magnificent plaid rug, the
practical solution was an informal two-part window treatment. The lower half of each window
is covered with shirred semisheer fabric, which admits light but screens the room from the gaze of
passersby, while the upper half is adorned with a simple length of yellow and white striped
fabric that falls gently from two medallion tiebacks to form a swag.

Below: Forming the backdrop for a plush velvet upholstered chair, round fringed pillow, and assorted Victorian oddments, including antler candlesticks, the bare wood trim around the window appeared underdressed and out of place. To dress up the corner quickly and without excessive fussing or measuring, a length of gold fabric was arranged into poufed gathers and tacked onto the trim. The fabric is tied into an oversize knot near the sconce, which effectively accentuates the opulent mood of the room.

Above: Streamlined and highly functional, standard white roller shades can look aesthetically stark and unfinished, especially when the decor is traditional rather than contemporary. To dress up the shades in this open-plan dining area, several yards of persimmon-colored fabric were threaded through rings across the top of the long window, then arranged into continuous swags. In addition to adding a color accent, the swagged fabric camouflages the shade hardware.

Below: As if twisted around a drapery pole by a mighty swirling wind, a length of chartreuse fabric fills this relatively straightforward dining area with tremendous energy and excitement. In contrast to the drapery's lively asymmetry, a vase of freshly cut flowers stands on a column pedestal in calm repose. The drapery's green cast does not interfere with the room's natural tones and makes a fitting prelude to the garden beyond.

Above: Striped curtains figure prominently in this dining area built around the three secondary colors—orange, green, and violet. Here, the walls and wood furnishings are orange in tone, the window muntins and woodwork are painted green, and the curtains and pillows contribute violet and blue hues as well as yellow accent stripes. An easy choice when a room is decorated with various colors, striped curtains can pull a room together and lend graphic interest as well.

49

~

Above: When dark furnishings and accessories create striking silhouettes against a white
wall, simple, unobtrusive curtains are in order. Here, long panels of nubby-textured
cotton drop to the floor from a black cast-iron pole. Blending in with the walls and woodwork,
the light, creamy color keeps the overall mood light and informal.

~

Left: Opening onto a private terrace, the fully glazed doors of this master bedroom
can be closed and voluminous draperies pulled shut over them. Designed with a reversible lining, the
draperies show yellow and white stripes to those inside the room, but appear gold when
viewed from outside. Spilling generously onto the floor, the drapery fabric conveys a mood of
pampered luxury and privilege in this spare but elegantly furnished room.

~

Above: When more daylight was desired at this seaside summer home, a piece of raffia made a handy and attractive tieback for a curtain panel, allowing a vacationer to get back to the serious business of rest and relaxation. The cotton fabric chosen for the curtain panel is serviceable, washable, and easily replaced if necessary, making maintenance a breeze.

~

Below: One of the beauties of older homes, glass-paned interior doors can be closed or opened as needed, depending on how often a room is used and on its traffic flow patterns. Here, an arm-chair placed in front of a closed door sends a definite no-exit signal, helping to make one end of the living room quieter and less of a thoroughfare. To prevent the room from becoming too cloistered, however, the door's rust-colored curtain is pulled to one side and secured with a tasseled rope. The arrangement allows light to pass back and forth, and preserves the home's airiness.

~

Below: A serene seashore view is enhanced by the simplicity of a gracefully draped swag at the window. Edged with a yellow trim that matches the striped wallpaper and chair upholstery, the delicate white swag provides a smooth visual transition between the bright room and a seascape that is foggy and overcast much of the year. The setting is so secluded that no additional curtains or shades are necessary.

53

~

Above: Adding a stylish note to an upstairs hallway, a printed scarf is draped off-center above a small window. The rectangular window ledge is deep, offering room for a potted plant that drinks in the sunlight while creating a natural privacy screen. Against the streaming sunlight, the scarf's dark print presents a moody, romantic contrast.

PART THREE

Windows of Opportunity

ONE-OF-A-KIND CREATIONS

transform eyesores like these, both artistically and affordably, making the least desirable element the pivotal point of a new, visually compelling design.

Decorating dilemmas that need resolving are but one route to novel curtain and drapery designs. For window treatments that are witty, daring, or visionary, you need to look inward to your own sense of drama and fantasy. The photographs featured in this section will help you look at the windows in your home in a new way. Here are curtains and drapes that go beyond the basic tasks of filtering the after-

*A*lmost every home has its unfortunate window flaws. A pair of windows that aren't quite symmetrical, an older home that has settled unevenly, or a boring stock window—all these imperfections can detract from the beauty of a home's interior. Successful window treatments noon sun or framing a garden view to truly express the heart and soul of a household. Bursting with inspiration, a playful spirit, and a love of make-believe, they prove that originality, rather than expense or pedigree, is the key to a home that pampers and delights.

~

Left: Instead of traditional curtains, triangles cut from old embroidered dinner napkins decorate the upper and lower sashes of this dining room window. Each piece is taken from a different napkin, producing a charming, eclectic effect. A few bottles of colored water and a frosted glass saucer complete this picture of days gone by.

~

Opposite: Overlooking an outdoor entry court, this foyer's window seat provides a bird's-eye view of a household's comings and goings. To screen the perch from outside eyes, a lace café curtain runs the length of the window, its fabric calling attention to white throw pillows plumped up on the seat cushion. Custom-made, yellow-striped Roman shades can be pulled down when the sunlight becomes too intense.

Below: When a less than attractive view must be tolerated in order to admit light into a room, a row of pretty plants on the windowsill can improve the situation. Here, paperwhite narcissus and small gardenias rise out of clay pots and almost touch the billowing hem of a lemon-colored balloon shade to draw attention away from the drab city landscape beyond. The shade's yellow cast is another decorating trick, as it makes the room appear sunny and bright, even on overcast days.

Above: Who says window treatments in a room have to match? The larger window in this living room was a candidate for vertical blinds, since it faces the street and receives a lot of direct sun throughout the day. Privacy was less of an issue at the smaller side window, so the blinds were omitted and a trio of potted plants were appropriated as a screen instead. Each window is topped by a uniquely shaped valance that was sewn from the same fabric used on the sofa and chairs.

~

Left: When draped across interior thresholds, curtains can give ordinary passage from one room to the next a sense of drama and anticipation. Here, a wide entry between a living room and dining room is made more intimate by the addition of long curtains secured at each side with ribbon tiebacks. Like curtains at a picture window, the gently sloping panels frame the dining area beyond and draw the eye toward it. When the tiebacks are released and the curtains are pulled closed, each room is converted into a private sanctuary.

57
~

Right: Any large, flat textile, such as a sheet, blanket, or tablecloth, is a candidate for becoming a curtain panel. This bedcover woven with serape-style stripes is a case in point. The panel fits the space without adjustments, and one of the hemmed edges forms a ready-made casing for the curtain rod. Two pieces of outsider art—a mask and a bottlecap-studded cross—help to complete the Southwestern look.

~

Below: In this room full of surprises, curtains appear almost everywhere but the windows! The owners of this home took advantage of its prewar architectural detail by hanging muslin panels from the wall's long picture-hanging moldings and creating the panels' soft folds with evenly spaced brass clips. In the midst of this roomy living and dining area, a gauzy mosquito netting envelops two facing love seats, making for an intimate conversation tent. Filling in for curtains, two potted topiaries are placed in front of each window, offering a pretty streetside welcome while safeguarding the room's privacy somewhat.

~

Above: In a striking optical illusion, draperies for two side-by-side windows appear to frame the narrow wall space between them. Painted a deep taupe, the wall provides a neutral backdrop for a favorite print. The pale apricot draperies offer an interesting contrast with the blues and reds of the furnishings. Long and lavish, the panels puddle on the floor, softening the hard angles of the furniture and pleated shades, too.

59
~

Below: Narrow orange trim is the common thread joining the many elements of this well-appointed living room. Showing most prominently as curtain tabs, which make a dynamic display grouped together on the fabric-covered curtain poles, the color orange also accents the side and lower hems of the curtain panels and the ruffled edge of a throw pillow. Even the four pictures hung between two of the curtain panels have warm natural wood frames that mimic the orange edging.

Above: Combining stripes of varying widths is a time-honored method of adding interest to a decor. In this living room, yellow and white striped wallpaper forms the backdrop for an upholstered sofa, love seat, and stool cushions as well as a host of decorative objects and accessories. The balloon shade's much narrower stripes, also yellow and white, are a foolproof addition to the lively mix. Echoing the shade's scalloped hem, a black and yellow striped swag border circles the room just below the ceiling molding.

Left: When a room is small, emphasizing special details or possessions can make the space seem cozy instead of cramped. In this dining nook, for example, deep red fabrics and an exotic mix of pictorial and geometric textile designs create an intimate, inviting atmosphere. To help the lace-curtained window relate more readily to the intense decor, an ornamental ironwork grille was set into the window frame. In keeping with the room's eclectic mix, a pretty flowering branch was encouraged to dangle into the space.

6 1

~

Above: In this contemporary home, sleek, metal-clad windows worked against the softer, more traditional mood the owner favored for the decor. Rather than try to remedy the situation with blinds or drapes, the misfit windows were bypassed altogether in favor of a folding oriental-style screen. Each section of the screen was fitted with a lace inset that graciously masks the offending windows, yet still admits daylight.

~

Left: When a room serves as a living room by day and a bedroom by night, the ideal decor must be alternately hospitable, seductive, and soporific. A white-on-white palette suits all three moods and is easily coordinated, from the seating to the bed linens. Here, filmy white draperies fall in gracious folds behind a cherry sofa that opens for sleeping. The French doors leading to the garden are left exposed during the day, but at night, the draperies close over them for complete privacy.

Right: In certain settings, leaving curtains out of the picture is the best option of all. For this novel kitchen renovation, glass-door cabinets were built against an existing window, providing a unique see-through view to the backyard. Since the cabinets are high on the wall, privacy is not compromised and no curtains are necessary. A few pieces of pottery displayed on the shelves keep the view simple and uncluttered.

64

Right: Mysteriously veiled with sheer, dark curtains, a bed becomes a private chamber within the larger room. Antique and contemporary, this self-styled bed mounts a wooden headboard and footboard on an aluminum four-poster frame that can be rolled around the room on rubber wheels. The curtains just skim the floor, giving the movable bed the appearance of a ghostly apparition.

~

Right: Looking much like the retracted awning outside a storefront, a pleated Roman shade dresses up an interior that is under renovation. Stripped of its original paint and now in a trial run of the new decor, the woodwork will eventually be painted white and feature meandering violets across all the pilasters. The green and white striped shade enhances the outdoor effect, and was put up by owners eager to visualize the final results.

Below: When a small room is big on windows, simplicity is the best rule of thumb to avoid a cluttered, cramped feeling. In this older home, the bathroom was inexplicably designed with two windows, each one nearly touching a side wall. Rather than fuss up the space with traditional shirred curtains, simple white roller shades appear solo over each window. To make the curtainless decor feel less austere, a painted design on the wall above adds a bit of swirl and drape to the setting.

Above: Set into a dormer alcove, a freestanding cast-iron tub is a romantic spot for lingering soaks. Quiet and understated, the decor features a checked window-seat cushion and a matching curtain with a pulled-up hem. As if to caress the bather, sheer white fabric drops down the side walls of the alcove before being caught up into graceful curves by long cord tiebacks.

~

Left: Functioning much like awnings, curtains that are hung outdoors can act as windbreaks, screen the sun's rays, or shelter porches from the driving rain. Here, a stately entry porch is flanked by two long curtain panels. Hung when the weather gets warm and put away during the chillier months, the curtains make the mansion seem less imposing and extend the hospitality of the interior rooms to the outdoor areas that are used for greeting and entertaining guests in the hotter months.

69

~

Left: Poolside dining under a portico takes on new elegance when draperies are installed within each Romanesque arch. In addition to making the portico feel more like an interior space, the white draperies help deflect the late afternoon sun.

Sources

~

Hardware, Hooks, and Tapes

There are many retail sources for curtain and drapery poles, rods, and brackets. These include hardware stores, discount and variety stores, home decorating centers, department stores, mail-order catalogs, and other vendors located in the telephone directory. For mail-order suppliers offering custom designs not sold elsewhere, try consulting the classified advertising section of home decorating magazines. Drapery hooks, tapes, and plastic rings as well as supplies for making shades are widely available, and can be found in hardware, home decorating, and sewing notions departments of many retail stores.

Shoppers often find the array of products related to curtain and drapery making staggering. If you have difficulty sorting out what you need, be sure to ask the store personnel to advise you. You may even want to devote a preliminary shopping excursion to examining and comparing the different possibilities and narrowing your choices. When you return to make a purchase, be sure to bring along your window and drapery sketches, including measurements, so that you can provide any details the store personnel might need to help you make your final selections.

Fabric and Sewing Supplies

Fabrics suitable for curtains and draperies are available at sewing supply stores, fabric stores, fabric departments in large retail stores, warehouse and mill end outlets, and by mail. You can identify fabric retailers in your area by consulting your local telephone directory. Mail-order sources can be found through advertisements in home decorating, fashion, and sewing magazines. Depending on where you shop, you may find bolts of fabric neatly arranged at eye level, rolls of fabric stacked three or four deep on wide shelves, or loose cuts of fabric in bins. Examine loose cuts carefully for flaws, such as pulled threads, tears, uneven dyeing, and so on, that will mar the finished panels. Sheers should be clean and free of snags. If you are planning a no-sew draped style, don't overlook lace tablecloths and printed sheets, which offer wide widths and prefinished edges. Again, bring along sketches with complete measurements and a small calculator when you shop, in case you need to do any last-minute figuring or want to double-check your arithmetic.

Additional sewing supplies, such as scissors, needles, pins, and thread, are readily available at mass merchandise stores, variety stores, and many fabric stores (though generally not at discount warehouse outlets, which specialize in fabric only). Larger department stores often stock drapery hooks, tapes, and rings, as well as no-sew drapery hardware, along with the sewing notions. Fabric shops catering to quilters are a good source for rotary cutters and accessories, and local shops often hold small classes and workshops to help beginners get started.

Design Ideas

Fresh, new design ideas for curtains and drapes abound in the pages of decorating magazines, home furnishings catalogs, and department store flyers. In fact, store displays featuring furniture, bedding, and linens are brimming with ideas and products to try in the home. Other sources include historic homes and museums, designer showcase houses (these homes are decorated by top designers and can be seen for an admission fee, which is donated to a charity), neighborhood house tours, and public places, such as restaurants and theaters, that rely on decor to attract clientele. Carry a small notebook with you so that you can make a rough sketch or jot down some of the details when you see a design that you like. You can study the sketch in more detail and develop the idea further at home.

Further Reading

The books listed below offer detailed illustrated instructions for making drapes, curtains, and shades that go beyond the scope of this book. Included are techniques on pleating panels by hand, for those who are interested in this aspect of drapery construction. Additional articles can be found in magazines specializing in a hands-on approach to home decor. A local public library can help you locate additional sources.

Curtains and Shades. Alexandria, Va.: Time-Life Books, 1985.

Curtains, Draperies & Shades. Menlo Park, Calif.: Lane Publishing Co., 1987 (a Sunset book).

Paine, Melanie. *Fabric Magic.* New York: Pantheon Books/Random House, Inc., 1987.

Singer Sewing Reference Library: Sewing for the Home. Minnetonka, Minn.: Cy DeCosse Incorporated in cooperation with the Singer Education Department, 1984.

Wilhide, Elizabeth. *Laura Ashley Windows.* New York: Harmony Books, 1988.

Photography Credits

Conversion Chart for Common Measurements

The following chart lists the approximate metric equivalents of inch measurements up to 20", rounded for practical use. To calculate equivalents not listed, multiply the number of inches by 2.54cm. To convert 36", for example, multiply 36 times 2.54, for an equivalent of 91.44cm, or 91.5cm when rounded.

½" = 1.3cm	5" = 12.5cm	9" = 23cm	13" = 33cm	17" = 43cm
1" = 2.5cm	6" = 15cm	10" = 25.5cm	14" = 35.5cm	18" = 45.5cm
2" = 5cm	7" = 18cm	11" = 28cm	15" = 38cm	19" = 48cm
3" = 7.5cm	8" = 20.5cm	12" = 30.5cm	16" = 40.5cm	20" = 51cm
4" = 10cm				

Index

~